NASHVILLE

A Picture Book to Remember Her By

CRESCENT BOOKS
NEW YORK

CLB 859
© 1987 Colour Library Books Ltd., Godalming, Surrey, England.
All rights reserved
This 1992 edition published by Crescent Books,
distributed by Outlet Book Company, a Random House Company
225 Park Avenue South, New York, New York 10003.
Printed and bound in Hong Kong
ISBN 0 517 47806 4
7 6 5 4 3 2 1

Even some of the most devoted fans of country music and the famous "Nashville Sound" may never have heard of a fiddler who called himself "Uncle Jimmy" Thompson. But he's clearly the grand daddy of the Sound.

One day in 1925, when Uncle Jimmy was 70 years old, he walked into the studios of Nashville's most powerful radio station, WSM, and offered to play for a spell. After an hour of playing, the announcer, George Dewey Hay, asked him if he didn't want to stop

"Heck no!," said Uncle Jimmy, "I'm just getting started. I played all night last night at a fair."

WSM's signal reached most of the eastern part of the country and calls began pouring in from as far away as Chicago and New York for more of Uncle Jimmy and folks like him. The station responded by adding a string band called "The Possum Hunters," and other groups with such names as "The Gully Jumpers" and "The Fruit Jar Drinkers."

The show just kept growing and people flocked to Nashville to be part of the studio audience. The station leased a movie theater to handle the crowds, then a former church and then a 3700-seat auditorium. But it still wasn't possible to get a seat less than a month in advance.

It wasn't long before the four-hour program became a staple on the coast-to-coast NBC network. One Saturday night, it followed a commercial announcement by the conductor Walter Damrosch for a program on grand opera. George Hay, who by then called himself "The Solemn Old Judge," and was the MC of the program, followed the announcement by telling his radio audience that "... you've just been up in the air with grand opera. Now get down to earth with us for a performance of Grand Old Opry."

That night, this beautiful city of Southern Colonial mansions, fine Victorian homes and some of the most beautiful gardens in the United States; the Capital of the great State of Tennessee, no less, gave America a new institution that has become as much a part of life in Southern California as in "Opryland" itself.

But it was the city that gave us Andrew Jackson, too. The hero of the Battle of New Orleans and America's seventh president gave the country a piece of Nashville flavor by reshaping the Federal Government along more populist lines. His friend Sam Houston was also a Nashville contribution to America's development. After having served Tennessee in the U.S. Congress, he became governor of the State before moving on to his destiny in Texas.

Nashville is the city that gave us Maxwell House Coffee, too. The dining room in the Maxwell House Hotel was considered the finest restaurant in the South for most of the second half of the 19th century. Its fame was spread when a local entrepreneur began marketing its coffee. Its fame was cemented in America's mind in 1907, when President Theodore Roosevelt was entertained to breakfast at Andrew Jackson's old homestead "The Hermitage."

"How did you like the coffee, Mr. President?" asked one of his Nashville hosts. "It was good to the last drop!" replied the president. It isn't every company that has a slogan coined by the Chief Executive himself.

But Nashville people have never needed outside help when it comes to choosing the right words. Early in the 19th century it earned the name "The Athens of The South" because its citizens were so obviously cultured and well-educated. It had its own theater presenting Shakespearean plays as early as 1850. And when P.T. Barnum took Jenny Lind there the following year, he said "there is far more female loveliness in Nashville than you will find in any other state in the Union." But you know old P.T. He said that to all the girls.

They began presenting grand opera (the real thing, the Italian kind) there in 1854. And a year later, the opening of the first public school in any Southern city confirmed that Nashville truly was "The Athens of The South."

But though the list of famous Nashville people runs from outlaw Jesse James to sportscaster Grantland Rice, the names most Americans associate with The Athens of The South are Eddy Arnold and Ernest Tubb, Minnie Pearl and Red Foley. The songs they gave us are such immortals as "Rabbit in The Pea Patch," "Late Last Night My Willy Came Home," and "Chittlin' Cookin' Time in Cheatham County." Older folks still smile over the antics of Lew Childre, the Boy From Alabam' and his sidekick Stringbean. And the younger generation is finding new inspiration, new things to smile about at Opryland, U.S.A.

In the process they're discovering other things to like about Nashville, U.S.A. It's been a progressive city since the beginning. It still follows the traditions of Andrew Jackson that every man has a chance to make something of himself. Men and women are proving it every day in Nashville.

Previous page: the national and state flags flutter above the State Capitol.
Facing page: the State Capitol.

Previous pages: the sparkling lights of the downtown area. Facing page and top: Deaderick Street and the columns of the War Memorial Building. Above: an exhibit from the Car Collectors Hall of Fame. Right: the Capitol.

Previous pages: the War Memorial Building and
State Capitol. These pages: Willie Nelson.
Overleaf: the view from the Victory Memorial
Bridge.

These pages: the Hermitage, home of President Jackson. Above: the log cabin in which the Jacksons lived until 1819. Top and facing page bottom: the Hermitage Mansion, which was extensively rebuilt in 1835 after a fire. Facing page top: the family graveyard, which includes the tomb of Andrew Jackson and his wife (right). Overleaf: the colorful lights of Music Row.

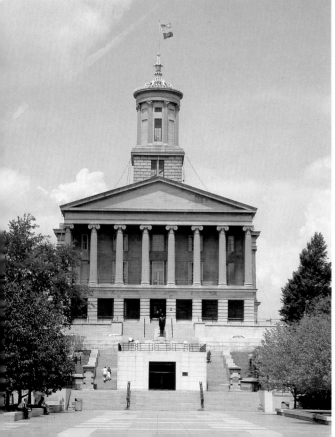

Top: the Country Music Hall of Fame and Museum. Left: the State Capitol. Above: the Municipal Auditorium. Facing page: the statue of President Andrew Jackson outside the State Capitol. Overleaf: Music Row.

Top and facing page top: the replica of the Parthenon in Athens, which graces Centennial Park. Left: St. Mary's Church is dominated by more modern buildings (above and facing page bottom). Overleaf: the Country Music Hall of Fame with (inset top left) Davidson County Public Building and Court House and (inset top right and inset bottom right) Music Row.

This page: Opryland USA, off Briley Parkway, combines country music with exciting rides. Facing page: the colorful signs of Printers Alley. Overleaf: Opryland Theater by the Lake.

These pages: the elegant Georgian mansion of Cheekwood. The 60-room house was once the home of Leslie Cheek and his family, but the house and the 55 acres of beautifully cared for gardens and buildings are now the home of the Tennessee Botanical Gardens and Fine Arts Center Inc. Overleaf: the Barbara Mandrell Country Store with (inset left) Davidson County Public Building and Court House and (inset right) the State Capitol and city center from Jefferson Street Bridge.

These pages: the Opryland Theater by the Lake, where open-air shows are staged for the benefit of visitors. Overleaf: the magnificent Doric colonnade of the War Memorial Building.

35

Built in 1853, Belle Meade was, until 1902, the acknowledged center of horse-breeding in the state: (top) the mansion; (left) the carriage house; (above) the stables and (facing page) a log cabin built in 1806. Overleaf: (top left and bottom right) the kitchen; (bottom left) the study and (top right) the dining room.

Previous pages: Deaderick Street. These pages: the colorful shops along Music Row. Overleaf: the Opryland Encore Theater.

Left: the springhouse at the Hermitage and (above) the nearby Tulip Grove, home of Andrew Jackson Donelson. Top and facing page: the recreated Fort Nashborough of 1780, in Riverfront Park. Overleaf: a truckstop on the interstate near downtown Nashville.

Top: the State Capitol at the head of Capitol Boulevard. Left: the War Memorial Building. Above: the view from the L&C Tower. Facing page: (top) 5th Avenue and (bottom) Deaderick Street.

Top left: Kenny Rogers. Top right: Don Williams. Left: Emmy Lou Harris. Above: Rita Coulidge. Facing page: (top left) Barbara Mandrell; (top right) Kris Kristofferson; (bottom left) Johnny Cash; (bottom right) Dolly Parton.

These pages: President Jackson's Hermitage.
Top: the parlor; (left) the entrance hall;
(above) the library; (facing page top) the
dining room and (facing page bottom) the
bedroom. Overleaf: Centennial Park.

57

Top: the Opryland Encore Theater. Left: a musician on Music Row. Above: Opryland Theater by the Lake. Facing page: Opryland Juke Box Theater.

Facing page: (left) Dolly Parton; (top right) Conway Twitty; (center right) Kenny Rogers; (bottom right) Emmy Lou Harris. Top: Johnny Cash. Above: Rita Coulidge. Right: Tammy Wynette.
Overleaf: Belmont Mansion.